Prentice Hall Regents ESL

MYSTERIES AND THE UNKNOWN

Overview

In *Mysteries and the Unknown,* children will explore the idea that we are surrounded by challenging, fascinating mysteries on Earth and in outer space. The fiction reading will help children appreciate the pleasures of using their intelligence and experience to solve mysteries in their everyday lives. The nonfiction reading will deepen children's appreciation for one of the ultimate mysteries of our universe—black holes. The magazine pages of Just for Fun will give children a chance to "travel" to some of Earth's mysterious places, to solve a riddle, and to evaluate the reliability of newspaper articles about mysterious occurrences.

Mysteries and the Unknown invites students to work with language related to crime investigation, scientific inquiry, and the world of the unexplained. Language structures include common and proper nouns, superlative forms of adjectives, and singular and plural possessive nouns. Students will develop skills needed to draw conclusions, paraphrase, and recognize cause and effect. Language functions in Everyday Talk include expressing annoyance, disbelief or surprise, speculation, and probability. Students' work will help them develop competency in English as they explore the mysteries of the universe.

Planning Ahead: The Theme Project

The suggested project for *Mysteries and the Unknown* is planning, creating, and presenting a panel discussion entitled "Mysteries: Solved and Unsolved." Begin the project by explaining that a panel discussion usually takes place among people seated at a long table. The panel members share information with one another and with an audience. Tell students that they will work in groups and that each group will have a panel discussion about a mystery they choose. Early in the theme encourage students to find out more about different mysteries that interest them. Stimulate students to think about mysteries as broadly as possible! Some children may be intrigued by mysteries having to do with people, places, or objects they know from their daily lives. Others may be interested in mysteries relating to history, the solar system, or nature. Arrange to have a volunteer record the panel discussions with a camcorder.

Getting Ready to Read

What Do Students Know?

Ask students if they have read books or seen movies about detectives and mysteries. Elicit as many details as possible. Then find out what students know about these topics:

▶ *Is crime bad? Yes or no?* (P)*

▶ *Do detectives commit crimes?* (EP)*

▶ *Why do we need police officers and detectives?* (SE)*

▶ *How do detectives solve crimes?* (NF)*

What Do Students Want to Know?

On chart paper, begin a continuum marked off to show the sequence of events in a mystery story. Elicit from students that a *mystery* is something that is difficult to explain or solve. Have them brainstorm (using their first language if necessary) and then express in English the steps that usually happen between the beginning and the end of the story. Invite volunteers to indicate where you should place their suggestions on the continuum. Ask students what else they would like to know.

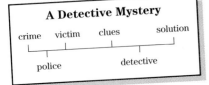

A Detective Mystery

crime   victim   clues   solution

         police   detective

Theme Presentation

OBJECTIVES

● **READING** To activate background knowledge/To use context clues to understand unfamiliar words

● **LISTENING/SPEAKING** To generate vocabulary needed to talk about solving a crime/To understand a narration based on visuals/To role-play or pantomime

KEY VOCABULARY

criminal, suspect, victim, chief of police, police officer, detective, crime, forgery, robbery, fake, mugging, commit, investigate, solve, rob, forge, mug, evidence, clue, fingerprint, check, money, handwriting

Introduce

▶ Display Transparency 1 and tell children that these drawings show four different places where crimes happened (*crime scenes*). Ask a volunteer to point out the detective in each scene.

▶ Have students listen while you describe each scene depicted on the page. Describe the elements of each picture, using the boxed vocabulary. To aid your less fluent students' comprehension, use gestures, act out, and rephrase ideas in several ways.

▶ Discuss the illustrations on page 2 and have children point to or talk about the pictures by responding to the following:

Point to the museum. (PREPRODUCTION)
Did someone rob the bank or rob the jewelry store? (EARLY PRODUCTION)
What evidence did one of the muggers leave behind? (SPEECH EMERGENCE)
What is happening in the second picture? (NEARLY-FLUENT)

▶ Have groups of students role-play or mime the crime scenes illustrated on page 2. After each improvisation, encourage the rest of the class to ask the actors *who, what, when, where, how,* and *why* questions.

Practice

Have students discuss each picture and answer the questions at the bottom of page 2. Make sure they identify the crime, the criminal, and the evidence in each scene.

Evaluate

Use Activity Page 1 to evaluate students' comprehension of the situations and new vocabulary. Students may work individually, in pairs, or in small groups. You may wish to take notes to help you track students' progress during the theme.

Preview • *The Case of the Secret Pitch*

OBJECTIVES

● **READING** To associate labels with locations/To match written words with pictures/To predict content from a story title/ To locate clues in a mystery story

● **LISTENING/SPEAKING** To describe a picture/To describe a location

● **WRITING** To record a mystery story

KEY VOCABULARY

agency, business, garage, store, house, railroad tracks, auto body shop, delicatessen, church, movie theater, bank, supermarket, elementary school, police station, encyclopedia, baseball, bat, pitch

Detectives solve mysteries and crimes. They investigate cases, look for clues and suspects, and gather evidence. Where is the detective's office? What other buildings are in town?

3

Vocabulary Preview

▶ Display Transparency 2. Invite students to find the detective. Students who locate him first can give clues to their classmates. (*He's near_____./He's to the right (left) of_____.*)

▶ Have children find and point to various locations in the town as you say aloud the names of the places. Ask them to repeat the names and tell what happens in each place.

▶ Ask students to describe the scene. As vocabulary words are mentioned, describe the place or the article, and point out key words on the transparency.

▶ Help students discuss the picture by asking questions, such as the following:

> *Where does the chief of police work? Show me.* (P)*
> *Is the bank near the railroad tracks or the shoe store?* (EP)*
> *How many stores are in this picture? What are they?* (SE)*
> *What is the detective doing in the picture?* (NF)*

▶ Ask students to name all the things on the transparency that have to do with baseball. Encourage them to tell what they know about the game of baseball.

Looking Ahead

Ask students if they think there is anything surprising about the detective in the story pictures. Some students may be familiar with Encyclopedia Brown. If so, invite them to tell what they know about the character. Then have students read the title of the book and look at the cover. Discuss the meaning of *case* ("a situation needing investigation") and have students predict the plot of the story.

> *Language Acquisition Levels: P = PREPRODUCTION; EP = EARLY PRODUCTION; SE = SPEECH EMERGENCE; NF = NEARLY-FLUENT

HOME–SCHOOL CONNECTION

Send home Activity Page 2, which suggests that a family member work with the child to record a mystery story from their home culture so that all the students can share their stories in class. You may wish to preview and classify their stories to prepare students for the range of mystery stories and crime-related mysteries that will be discussed.

Rereading for Different Purposes

Students will probably benefit from repeated readings of *The Case of the Secret Pitch*. To vary the readings and help children understand difficult concepts in the story, encourage them to set different purposes:

▶ The audio cassette presents an original selection that guides students through the elements of a mystery story. After students listen to the story, have them either write a summary or create an illustrated story strip.

▶ Encourage children to reread the story so they can find the clues that made Encyclopedia Brown certain that the letter and the check were fakes.

▶ Some students may enjoy getting together to make their own recording of the story.

Reading the Literature

The Case of the Secret Pitch

READING STRATEGIES / CRITICAL THINKING SKILLS

● Recognizing cause and effect
● Noting details
● Deducing
● Paraphrasing or summarizing

OBJECTIVES

● **READING** To predict character and plot from illustrations/To use context clues to understand unfamiliar words/To draw conclusions
● **LISTENING/SPEAKING** To recognize and use appropriate gestures, facial expressions, and intonation
● **WRITING** To speculate about a story's ending/To narrate a past experience

Introduce

Have students work in small groups to create diagrams of a baseball field. Provide large pieces of paper, markers, and rulers. Have students label the four bases (first base, second base, third base, home plate), the pitcher's mound, the infield, and the outfield. Ask them to use their diagrams to demonstrate what happens when a player is at bat, a batter hits a single (double/triple/home run), a runner takes a long lead off base, and so on. They may use stick-on notes or checkers to represent the players.

Read

▶ This selection will be challenging because students will not be able to rely on the illustrations to provide help in following the details of the plot. You may wish to approach the reading in the following manner: First, ask students to read each page silently. Then ask for volunteers to read each page aloud as the rest of the class follows along.

▶ After reading each page, ask children to give the main idea or to paraphrase or summarize what happened. Afterwards or on another reading, you may wish to discuss more detail and to call attention to selected language points.

On This Page

▶ Show students an encyclopedia volume. Ask what an encyclopedia contains and for what purposes students could use it. Then ask why a person might be called Encyclopedia. If they aren't sure, tell them to look for the answer as they read on.

▶ If necessary, explain that Sherlock Holmes is a famous English detective created by Arthur Conan Doyle. Make sure that children understand that the author of the story is suggesting that Encyclopedia Brown (like Holmes) is the best detective in his country.

▶ Ask students to identify some laws. Explain that *breaking a law* means "doing what the law says not to do."

Language Focus

● **Common and proper nouns**
● **Superlative forms of adjectives**

▶ After children read, you may want to help them understand that there are two kinds of nouns—common nouns and proper nouns. Common nouns name general words and are not capitalized. Proper nouns name specific people, places, and things and are always capitalized. Ask students to scan these pages for common and proper nouns.

ENCYCLOPEDIA BROWN

THE CASE OF THE Secret Pitch
by Donald J. Sobol

Idaville looked like any other town of its size—from the outside.

On the inside, however, it was different. Ten-year-old Encyclopedia Brown, America's Sherlock Holmes in sneakers, lived there.

Besides Encyclopedia, Idaville had three movie theaters, a Little League, four banks, and two delicatessens. It had large houses and small houses, good schools, churches, stores, and even an old section by the railroad tracks....

And it had, everyone believed, the best police force in the world.

For more than a year no one—boy, girl, or grown-up—had got away with breaking a single law.

4 Mysteries and the Unknown

▶ Tell students that to compare more than two people or things, they should use the *-est* ending with most adjectives. Point out that instead of the *-est* ending, the word *most* is used before longer adjectives. Introduce the irregular forms *good/better/best* and *bad/worse/worst.* Have children find examples of superlative forms on pages 4 and 5. *(best, smartest, best trained, bravest, hardest)*

Meeting Individual Needs

REINFORCEMENT

☒ You may wish to have *kinesthetic* learners act out the confrontation scenes in the clubhouse on pages 10–12. Less fluent students might take the nonspeaking parts, and more fluent students might write a script or play major roles.

BUILDING SELF-ESTEEM

Baseball is no longer the national pastime of only the U.S. To underline that point, students from other cultures, such as Mexico, Cuba, Puerto Rico, South America, and Japan, might enjoy presenting what they know about the game. Invite them to work in small groups to prepare presentations about special pitching, hitting, or fielding tips that interest them.

CHALLENGE

Suggest that students read other stories by Donald J. Sobol that feature Encyclopedia Brown. Encourage them to describe the plots of these stories to the class.

Encyclopedia's father was chief of police. People said he was the smartest chief of police in the world and his officers were the best trained and the bravest. Chief Brown knew better.

His men were brave, true enough. They did their jobs well. But Chief Brown brought his hardest cases home for Encyclopedia to solve.

For a year now Chief Brown had been getting the answers during dinner in his red brick house on Rover Avenue. He never told a soul. How could he?...

Encyclopedia never let out the secret, either. He didn't want to seem different from other fifth-graders.

5

On This Page

▶ Help children understand the differences in the terms *chief of police, officer,* and *detective.* Have volunteers explain the different duties and levels of skill required to perform each of these jobs.

▶ Point out the expression *never told a soul.* Have children guess from the context that this means that the chief "never told any other person."

Cross-Curricular Connections

SCIENCE

Ask students whether they know what a baseball is made of. Provide them with an inexpensive baseball. (Perhaps the physical education department can contribute a worn-out one.) Help students take the baseball apart carefully in order to discover that it is made of cork, rubber, yarn, rubber cement, cowhide, and red cotton stitching. They might do further research to find how its materials facilitate movement during a baseball game.

SOCIAL STUDIES

The Federal Bureau of Investigation (FBI) solves thousands of mysteries and crimes in the U.S. each year. Have an interested group of students read about the FBI in an encyclopedia and then "brief" the rest of the class by presenting the information they find.

MUSIC/MULTICULTURAL

Play recordings of instrumental and popular music that suggest an atmosphere of mystery. (This music might include the themes from TV's *The Twilight Zone*, from the theater's *The Phantom of the Opera*, or from the soundtracks of mystery movies and plays.) Invite students to think of musical instruments (as well as particular tunes) from their home cultures that sound mysterious in tone. If they do not name the organ, tubular bells, cello, oboe, gong, musical saw, and the human voice itself, tell them that those instruments have been used to convey a sense of mystery.

Mainstream Connections

Students may want to share *The Case of the Secret Pitch* with mainstream friends and have them try to solve the case.

On This Page

- ▶ Ask a volunteer to explain what a nickname is. Make sure that students understand how Encyclopedia got his nickname.
- ▶ Have students tell nicknames they are familiar with in English or in their first languages. Ask them to speculate about why many sports figures have nicknames.
- ▶ As they continue to read, students should identify nicknames of other characters and speculate about how the characters might have gotten them.

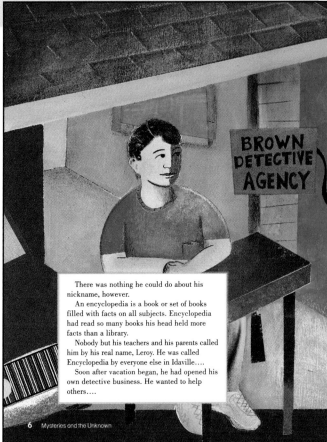

There was nothing he could do about his nickname, however.

An encyclopedia is a book or set of books filled with facts on all subjects. Encyclopedia had read so many books his head held more facts than a library.

Nobody but his teachers and his parents called him by his real name, Leroy. He was called Encyclopedia by everyone else in Idaville....

Soon after vacation began, he had opened his own detective business. He wanted to help others....

6   Mysteries and the Unknown

Language Focus

● **Comparisons with nouns**

▶ Call students' attention to the last sentence in the second paragraph on page 6. Ask what the author is comparing. *(Encyclopedia's head and a library)* Then ask what they have in common. *(Both contain a lot of facts.)*

▶ Ask students which source has a greater quantity of facts, according to the author. You may use a formula to help students understand: [name/ noun] has more/less [noun] than [person/thing]. Invite students to tell something special about themselves using a similar comparison with nouns.

Everyday Talk

● **Asking for help**

▶ Point out that in the story Speedy asks Encyclopedia for help simply by saying, "I need help." Elicit from students other expressions that he could have used, such as the following:

Could you please help me _____?
Would you help me _____?
Help! I need _____.

▶ Have students brainstorm situations in which they might ask for help and then work with partners to role-play their exchanges in these situations.

On This Page

Demonstrate the expression *to wear a long face.* Elicit from students the feeling that goes with your facial expression. *(sadness)* Then discuss the idea that the *last day of school* feels very long to some students. Ask a volunteer to put the two phrases together and tell the meaning of "He wore a face longer than the last day of school." *(Speedy looked very sad.)*

One morning Speedy Flanagan, the shortest fast-ball pitcher in the Idaville Little League, walked into the Brown Detective Agency. He wore a face longer than the last day of school.

"I need help," he said…. "What do you know about Browning?…

The American League pitcher, Robert *Spike* Browning."…

Everyday Talk

- **Expressing confusion**
- **Asking for clarification**

▶ Explain that people may paraphrase, or restate something in different words, when they want the speaker to clarify or simplify or change the tempo of his or her speech. Ask a volunteer to find the sentence on page 8 where Encyclopedia paraphrases Speedy's words.

▶ Ask students what word tells them that Encyclopedia wants Speedy to slow down. *(Whoa!)* You may want to demonstrate appropriate intonation, expression, and gestures.

▶ Have students brainstorm to recall situations in which they have not understood someone. Elicit expressions that can be used to express confusion, and list them on the board. Categorize according to whether the language can be used with friends or with adults:

Friends: *Whoa! Wait a minute! Slow down! What did you say?*

Adults: *I'm sorry. I don't understand./Could you repeat that?/Would you say that again?*

Theme Poster

On This Page

▶ Help students see that Bugs's secret pitch has a name: a "cross-eyed special." Ask volunteers to study the drawing and then demonstrate how a person might throw a pitch called a cross-eyed special.

▶ Clarify for children that Encyclopedia, Speedy, and Bugs all live in Idaville and that Bugs and his father traveled to New York City. Help students understand the inference that Spike Browning plays baseball in New York. Ask whether any of them ever visited New York City or know about New York baseball teams.

"What do you want to know about him?" asked Encyclopedia.

"Do you know what his handwriting looks like?" asked Speedy. "I made a bet with Bugs Meany—my bat against his—that Bugs couldn't get Spike Browning to buy a secret pitch for a hundred dollars."

"Whoa!" cried Encyclopedia. "If I understand you, Bugs bet he could sell Spike Browning a special way to throw a baseball?"

"Right. Bugs and his father were in New York City the last week in June," said Speedy. "Bugs says he sold Spike Browning his cross-eyed special."

"You'd better explain," said Encyclopedia.

8　Mysteries and the Unknown

Language Focus

● *Had better*

▶ Call students' attention to the last line on page 8. Tell them that Encyclopedia is giving Speedy some advice. Ask them why Encyclopedia suggests to Speedy that he explain what he means.

▶ Point out that the expression *had better* is used before the simple form of a verb and denotes giving advice to, recommending, or suggesting. (You may want to remind students that *had* becomes *'d* when used with subject pronouns, as in *I'd* and *you'd*.)

WRITER'S JOURNAL

Explain to students that Encyclopedia and Speedy seem to agree that Bugs is a suspect. Ask them whether they agree or disagree with Encyclopedia and Speedy. Have students record their ideas and their reasons in their journals.

HOME-SCHOOL CONNECTION

Encourage students to read a mystery story in English or in their home language with a family member.

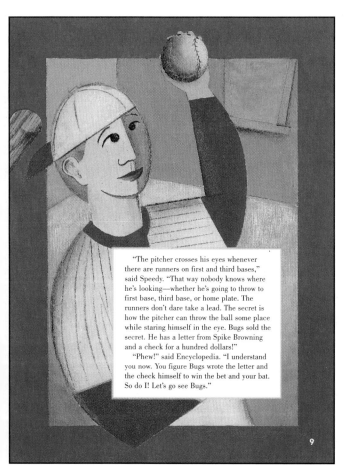

"The pitcher crosses his eyes whenever there are runners on first and third bases," said Speedy. "That way nobody knows where he's looking—whether he's going to throw to first base, third base, or home plate. The runners don't dare take a lead. The secret is how the pitcher can throw the ball some place while staring himself in the eye. Bugs sold the secret. He has a letter from Spike Browning and a check for a hundred dollars!"

"Phew!" said Encyclopedia. "I understand you now. You figure Bugs wrote the letter and the check himself to win the bet and your bat. So do I! Let's go see Bugs."

9

On This Page

▶ Ask students whether they have ever played in or attended a baseball game. Invite knowledgeable volunteers to act out various parts of the game, showing the meanings of *pitch, fastball, hit, catch, swing,* and *taking a lead*.

▶ Using the diagrams the students made in the Introduce section on page 4, clarify the situation Speedy is describing: *A pitcher is prepared to pitch the ball to the batter.* Runners are at first and third base. A pitcher could throw to third base or first base, trying to get either of those runners tagged out, or he could throw to the batter at home plate. According to Speedy, the runners and the batter are confused when the pitcher crosses his eyes—they don't know what he plans to do. Thus the runners don't dare step away from the bases (*take a lead*).

▶ Mime Encyclopedia saying "Phew!" at the end of Speedy's explanation. Ask what Encyclopedia is feeling when he says this. (*relief, understanding*)

Story Card 1

- **Singular and plural possessive nouns**
  ▶ Explain that nouns can show ownership. Discuss the idea that a singular possessive noun contains an apostrophe and the letter *s*. Ask students to find examples on this page. *(Friday's, Mr. Sweeney's)*
  ▶ Explain to students that a plural possessive noun is usually formed by adding an apostrophe. Have students find the example on page 10. *(Tigers')*

On These Pages

▶ You may want to point out the term *itching powder* and explain that some people confuse *itching* with *scratching*. Ask a volunteer to tell the difference. After you have helped students understand the comparison between itching powder and Bugs' gang, ask them what the comparison tells about the Tigers.

▶ To develop an understanding of *auto body*, point out that the word *body* can be used to refer to a person, an animal, or a thing.

▶ Clarify the meaning of *sole rights* by explaining that Spike is the only one with whom Bugs will share his secret. (You may wish to compare the spelling of *sole* with that of *soul* on page 5 and identify these words as *homonyms*, or words that sound alike but are spelled differently.)

▶ Ask a student who is a baseball fan to explain *spitball* or to mime what the pitcher does to deliver a spitball. Point out that spitballs are not allowed (are illegal) in baseball, and ask students why they think spitballs are against the rules.

▶ Explain the meaning of *drawn on the First National Bank* by telling students that people deposit money in a bank. When they want or need their money, they can *draw on it*, or take it out of the bank. If possible, show students a blank personal check and explain its parts.

Bugs Meany was the leader of the Tigers, a gang of older boys who caused more trouble than itching powder in Friday's wash. Since setting up as a detective, Encyclopedia had stopped many of Bugs' shady deals.

The Tigers' clubhouse was a tool shed behind Mr. Sweeny's Auto Body Shop. When Encyclopedia and Speedy arrived,... the Tigers' leader said, "Get lost."

"Not until I have a chance to see the letter and check from Spike Browning," said Encyclopedia.

Bugs opened a cigar box and passed Encyclopedia a check and a letter. Encyclopedia read the letter.

10 Mysteries and the Unknown

Theme Project Update

After students finish reading and discussing *Encyclopedia Brown and the Case of the Secret Pitch,* encourage them to think about ways to use what they learned to prepare their videotaped panel presentation. Ideas might include the following:

▶ Present information about famous detectives and famous criminals in history and in literature.

▶ Interview a local police detective about his or her work.

▶ Create a mystery to present to an audience whose members might be willing to participate in solving the case.

The letter was written on plain white paper. The check, bearing the same date as the letter, was drawn on the First National Bank for one hundred dollars.

▶ Ask children to find and copy existing illustrations of Sherlock Holmes or to create their own representations of him and other famous detectives.

▶ Ask students to create a TV advertisement that a private detective or a detective agency might broadcast. Encourage them to think about the qualities and talents that detectives would wish to emphasize.

Everyday Talk

● **Expressing annoyance**

▶ Ask students what expression on page 10 shows that Bugs does not want Encyclopedia and Speedy in the clubhouse. *(Get lost.)*

▶ Help students develop a list of expressions they can use when someone annoys them. *(Examples: Stop it!/Leave me alone!/ Be quiet!/ Go away!)* Help them understand in what situations these expressions are appropriate.

▶ You may want to lead a discussion of problems children sometimes have with bullies, whether they are older siblings, neighbors, or other students. Have students brainstorm strategies for dealing with "trouble" and for avoiding confrontations. Help them learn expressions they can recall to defend themselves verbally in difficult situations.

What Did Students Learn?

Invite children to look at the continuum they began before they read the story and add what they have learned.

WRITER'S JOURNAL

Have students describe a time when they acted like a "detective" and looked for explanations for mysterious events, including something so simple as finding out who borrowed a pair of sneakers or what happened to the last cookie in a package.

After You Read

Post-Reading Activities

OBJECTIVES

● **READING** To sequence story events/To analyze plot

● **LISTENING/SPEAKING** To role-play/To give details about story events/To summarize the plot of a story

● **WRITING** To write an advertisement/To write a letter

Vocabulary Check

▶ Use Story Card 1 to encourage students to use vocabulary relating to detectives and crime.

▶ After you form students into groups, have them stage a "crime investigation" in the classroom. The groups will plan a "robbery" or other crime and plant plenty of evidence around the scene of the crime. Then the groups will alternate in investigating one another's crimes. During the investigations, encourage students to use vocabulary they learned while reading the story.

Comprehension Check

Invite students to talk about the pictures on page 13. Then ask for a volunteer to read each sentence aloud. Encourage less fluent speakers to point to the appropriate picture after each sentence is read. Ask a volunteer to read the directions to the class. The class will then reread the six sentences to discover which one tells what came first in the story. *(sentence 4)* Then have students reorganize the remaining sentences. *(2,3,5,1,6)* Suggest that students look back at the story to verify the sequence.

Practice

Write the following sentences on separate slips of paper. Form the class into pairs or groups and have each group choose a slip. Invite each group to make a drawing of its events on chart paper:

▶ Bugs and Speedy make a bet.
▶ Bugs writes a fake check and letter.
▶ Speedy goes to see Encyclopedia, asking for help.
▶ Speedy explains the bet, the letter, and the check.
▶ Speedy and Encyclopedia go to see Bugs.
▶ Encyclopedia examines the letter and the check.
▶ Encyclopedia tells Bugs the letter and the check are fakes.

When all the events have been illustrated, have students place the pages in chronological order and tell about each event.

On This Page

▶ Explain that the word *man* is used on page 12 in a slang expression, *man, oh man!* This phrase expresses disbelief or frustration. Ask whether students know any other slang expressions in English or in their home languages that mean the same as this one.

▶ Make sure students can distinguish between a *baseball season* and the seasons of the year. Have a volunteer tell when the baseball season usually begins and ends in the U.S. *(April to October)*

Looking Back at the Story

Discuss how Encyclopedia solved the crime by focusing on the date of the letter. Make sure students realize that there are 30 days in June, not 31. You may wish to teach the following rhyme:

Thirty days has September,
April, June, and November.
All the rest have thirty-one,
Except for February fine,
Which has only twenty-eight
Till leap year gives it twenty-nine.

Display a calendar as you discuss this rhyme.

"Spike will win fifty games this season," said Bugs. "And I won one baseball bat from Speedy Flanagan. So where is it?"

"Where's *your* bat?" corrected Encyclopedia. "Speedy won the bet. You lost. The letter and check are fakes."...

"Man, oh man!" sang Bugs. "I invented the greatest pitch since Edison threw out the gas lamp. No smart-aleck private detective is going to walk in here and call me a liar!"

"Oh, yes I am," said Encyclopedia. "Spike Browning never wrote that letter. That check is a worthless piece of paper!"

WHAT MADE ENCYCLOPEDIA
SO CERTAIN?...

Evaluate

On the chalkboard, write a series of questions—the answers to which will form a "story chain." *(See illustration.)* Read each question aloud. Then form students into six small groups and assign each group one question to answer. Encourage students to scan the story to find or verify their answers. Have one volunteer from each group read aloud their assigned question. Then have other group members use gestures, pantomime, or detailed sentences to answer the question. You may wish to paraphrase some comments to help less fluent students understand the answers. Write the answers next to the questions on the board so that students can follow the "story chain." You may want to have volunteers point out which event took place *first, next,* and *last* in order to practice sequencing.

After You Read

Read each sentence. The sentences are not in the right order. On a separate piece of paper, write the sentences in the correct order.

1. Bugs shows Speedy and Encyclopedia a letter and a check from Spike Browning.
2. Encyclopedia learns that Bugs and Speedy made a bet with each other.
3. Bugs says that he sold his idea for a special pitch. He says that the American League pitcher Spike Browning bought his idea.
4. Encyclopedia opens his own detective agency.
5. Speedy and Encyclopedia think that Bugs made up the story about Spike because he wanted to win the bet.
6. Encyclopedia tells Bugs that the check and the letter are fakes. He says that Speedy has won the bet.

13

Story chain questions:

- Who runs a detective business in the story?
- Who comes to this detective for help?
- Which two people make a bet?
- What is a "cross-eyed special"?
- What evidence suggests that Bugs Meany is not telling the truth?
- How does the detective know the evidence is fake?

WRITER'S CORNER

Beginning

● **To write an advertisement**

PRE-WRITE: Invite groups of students to design magazine advertisements announcing the services of Encyclopedia Brown. Provide samples of different ads. Students may first wish to brainstorm to develop a list of Encyclopedia's talents and accomplishments. WRITE: Drawing on their list, students will write one or two sentences to use in their advertisements.

Remind them that these sentences should tell what makes Encyclopedia Brown a good detective. REVISE, EDIT: Encourage classmates to look at the advertisements and offer suggestions. Have students make revisions as necessary. Then have them copy the revised text and add illustrations or other design features to their work. PUBLISH: Display the finished advertisements.

Intermediate and Advanced

● **To write a letter**

PRE-WRITE: Encourage students to think about real or imaginary mysteries they would like to write and send to Encyclopedia Brown. Use the letter on page 11 as a model to help them identify the parts of a letter. *(heading, salutation, body, closing, signature)* WRITE: Have more fluent and less fluent students work in pairs to write their letters. Remind them to check that they have included all the parts of a letter. REVISE, EDIT: Have pairs exchange letters and make suggestions for improvements. Then have the original pairs revise their letters based on the suggestions they've received. PUBLISH: Collect letters and responses in an album and add it to the classroom library.

For coordinating activities, see the CD-ROM disk that corresponds with this theme.

Getting Ready to Read

What Do Students Know?

Tell students that there are many natural mysteries on Earth and in space. Elicit some examples from them. Then use the following questions to find out what students know about these mysteries:

▶ *Where is the sky? Show me.* **(P)***

▶ *Are you more interested in things on Earth or in space?* **(EP)***

▶ *What interesting places on Earth have you seen?* **(SE)***

▶ *When you look at the night sky, what do you wonder about?* **(NF)***

What Do Students Want to Know?

Tell students that they are going to read about a mystery in space called black holes. To find out what students want to know about the subject of black holes, develop a question tree on chart paper and have them suggest questions about outer space.

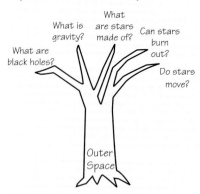

Have volunteers read aloud the questions and circle those that they would like to know the answers to.

Theme Presentation

OBJECTIVES

● **READING** To match written words with illustrations/To activate background knowledge

● **LISTENING/SPEAKING** To role-play/To contribute to a round-robin story

● **WRITING** To write dialogue

KEY VOCABULARY

marine biologist, observe, take notes, archaeologist, camera, ruins, heat, dig, geologist, ground, cold, test, astronomer, telescope, sky, observatory, ocean, desert, Arctic, space, Earth, interesting, place

Introduce

▶ Display Transparency 3 and explain to students that the four illustrations show scientists studying the mysteries of four different places. Have volunteers use the captions to name the places.

▶ Read aloud the words in the box and help volunteers point out the objects in the pictures. Then have students tell what the scientists might want to find out in each place.

▶ Encourage volunteers to describe what they see in each picture by asking questions such as the following:

Point to a hot place. **(PREPRODUCTION)**
In the Arctic, is it hot or cold? **(EARLY PRODUCTION)**
What mystery are the scientists studying in the desert? **(SPEECH EMERGENCE)**
What mysteries of space would you like to explore? **(NEARLY-FLUENT)**

▶ Have students imagine that they are scientists working in one of the four environments. Have partners tell what they

might see in their environment and role-play their work in actions and words.

Practice

Have pairs work on Activity Page 3. Partners can help each other complete the speech balloons. You may want to pair students from similar language backgrounds.

Evaluate

Use Activity Page 3 to evaluate informally. Have students read their completed sentences to the whole group. Then suggest that they use the pictures to make up a round-robin story. As you point to a student, he or she should expand the story until you point to another student. Some students may need to act out their parts of the story.

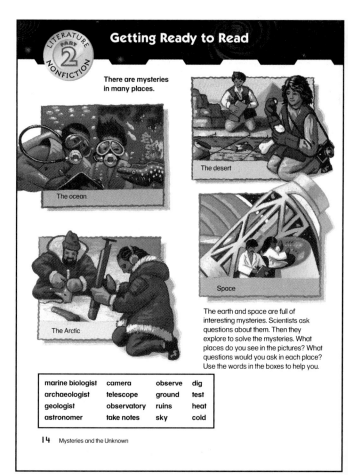

Getting Ready to Read

There are mysteries in many places.

The ocean

The desert

The Arctic

Space

The earth and space are full of interesting mysteries. Scientists ask questions about them. Then they explore to solve the mysteries. What places do you see in the pictures? What questions would you ask in each place? Use the words in the boxes to help you.

marine biologist	camera	observe	dig
archaeologist	telescope	ground	test
geologist	observatory	ruins	heat
astronomer	take notes	sky	cold

14   Mysteries and the Unknown

Preview • *The Mystery of Black Holes*

OBJECTIVES

● **READING** To predict content from illustrations
● **LISTENING/SPEAKING** To describe a picture/To participate in a group discussion/ To relate background knowledge

KEY VOCABULARY

planet, moon, gravity, star, sun, rays, astronaut, spaceship, bigger, smaller, light, darkness, shine, swirl, float, black hole

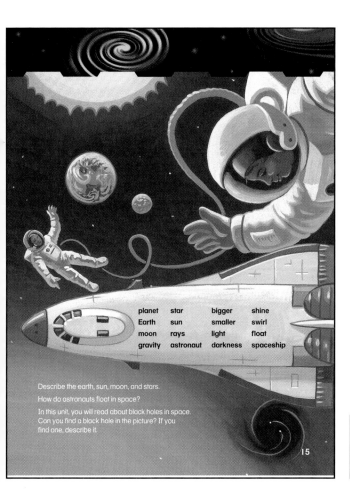

planet	star	bigger	shine
Earth	sun	smaller	swirl
moon	rays	light	float
gravity	astronaut	darkness	spaceship

Describe the earth, sun, moon, and stars.

How do astronauts float in space?

In this unit, you will read about black holes in space. Can you find a black hole in the picture? If you find one, describe it.

15

Vocabulary Preview

▷ Have students pretend that they are looking at the sky on a clear night. Encourage volunteers to imagine what they might see. Invite students to share their ideas orally or through pantomime.

▷ Have students look at Transparency 4. Help them discuss the illustration by asking questions such as the following:

Where is the planet Earth? **(P)***
Does the sun give off light? **(EP)***
What can an astronaut see through the window of the spaceship? **(SE)***
Why do astronauts explore space? **(NF)***

▷ Have students point to various objects and sights in the picture as you say the corresponding words aloud. Then reverse roles and have students say the words as you point to the objects or sights in the illustration.

▷ Have groups of students work on page 15. Ask them to discuss the questions at the bottom of the page and report ideas back to the class.

▷ Write the term *black holes* on the board and explain that black holes constitute one big mystery of space. Ask students what they know about black holes. Tell them that they will be reading to find out what scientists think black holes are.

Looking Ahead

Have students study the illustrations in the selection and tell what they see in space. Then point out there are some things in space that no one can see, even with the help of a strong telescope. Ask volunteers what some of these things might be.

* Language Acquisition Levels: P = PREPRODUCTION; EP = EARLY PRODUCTION; SE = SPEECH EMERGENCE; NF = NEARLY-FLUENT

HOME–SCHOOL CONNECTION

Encourage students to ask family members to share stories about the heavens and outer space from their cultures. These stories may be about myths or well-known scientific discoveries. Also, urge students to visit a local planetarium or science museum with their families. Note: For additional materials on outer space, you may want to use story cards, transparencies, or posters from *Sun, Moon, Earth, Stars* (Set I) and *Beyond the Earth* (Set II).

Rereading for Different Purposes

You may choose to have the children do multiple, repeated readings of *The Mystery of Black Holes* while listening to the audio tape. To vary the readings, help them set different purposes, such as the following:

▷ **Reread** *The Mystery of Black Holes* to find out how gravity affects things differently in different places.

▷ **Reread** the selection to compile a list of different facts about light.

Reading the Literature

The Mystery of Black Holes

READING STRATEGIES
CRITICAL THINKING SKILLS

- Role-playing
- Visualizing
- Paraphrasing
- Comparing and contrasting

OBJECTIVES

- **READING** To recognize homophones/To identify sentence types
- **LISTENING/SPEAKING** To participate in a quiz show/To use appropriate intonation
- **WRITING** To compose song lyrics/To write about an imaginary situation

Introduce

▶ If possible, distribute a flashlight to each pair of students. First, have them play with the light. Then ask them to shine it on a wall. Point out how light bounces off walls. Have students experiment with shining the light on a piece of clear plastic wrap to see how it passes through the plastic wrap. Then have students shine the light onto a piece of dark fabric to see how the light appears to be sucked in. Encourage discussion on the part of the two partners. Then have the whole class compare observations.

▶ Review the names of colors, such as *black, white, blue, green, yellow, red, violet,* and *orange.*

Read

▶ As you proceed through the story, help students visualize and act out the ideas. The story contains many opportunities for *kinesthetic* or *visual* learning (with words such as *squashed, tightly, gravity, bounce*).

▶ After students read each page, help them paraphrase the descriptions, facts, and ideas on the page. As they work, encourage them to circle additional questions on the question tree and to add questions as their knowledge increases.

On This Page

▶ If possible, bring a small telescope to class and demonstrate its use. Invite students to experiment with the telescope by looking at objects inside and outside the classroom.

▶ Point out the word *sparkling* and illustrate its meaning by showing students several things that sparkle, such as jewelry, shiny metal, and glass. (You may want to have students shine a flashlight on those objects to accentuate their sparkle.)

Language Focus

- **Expressions of quantity**
- **Prefix *in-***

▶ Have students find expressions that tell how many. (*a lot, some, even more, many*) Point out that these expressions are used when someone does not know the exact number. Invite students to speculate about exactly how many stars are "a lot."

▶ Help students pronounce *invisible.* Show children that adding *in-* to *visible* changes the meaning to "something we can't see." Have them define other words that begin with *in-.* (*Examples: incomplete/not complete, indirect/not direct*)

LITERATURE PART 2 NONFICTION

THE MYSTERY OF BLACK HOLES
by Billy Aronson

How many things can you see in the night sky? A lot! On a clear night you might see the moon, some planets, and thousands of sparkling stars.

You can see even more with a telescope. You might see stars where before you only saw dark space. You might see that many stars look larger than others. You might see that some "white" stars are really red or blue.

With bigger and bigger telescopes you can see more and more things in the sky. And you can see those things in more and more detail.

But scientists believe there are some things in the sky that we will never see. We won't see them with the biggest telescope in the world, on the clearest night of the year.

That's because they're invisible. They're the mysterious dead stars called black holes.

16 Mysteries and the Unknown

Meeting Individual Needs

REINFORCEMENT

▶ *Kinesthetic* learners may enjoy acting out some of the actions described in the story, such as *pull toward the center*, *squash inward*, *pull down*, *suck in*, *bounce back*, *swirl around one another*, *give off*, and *stretch*. Have students draw action words at random from a bag and play charades.

▣ Arrange students from each level of language acquisition into small, heterogeneous groups. Have each group make up three questions based on the selection and write them on index cards. Collect the cards and use them as the basis for a "quiz show." Assign the roles of contestants, emcee, scorekeeper, and judges according to students' interests and learning styles.

BUILDING SELF-ESTEEM

If possible, take children on a field trip to a science museum or planetarium. After the trip, encourage them to visit the place again with siblings or friends in other classes, pointing out exhibits they found particularly interesting.

CHALLENGE

Encourage more fluent speakers to learn more about the sky and outer space by reading *The Super Science Book of Space* by Jerry Wellington (Thomson Learning, 1993) and *The Space Atlas* by Heather Couper and Nigel Henbest (Gulliver Books/ Harcourt Brace, 1992).

You might find it hard to imagine that stars die. After all, our sun is a star. Year after year we see it up in the sky, burning brightly, giving us light and heat. The sun certainly doesn't seem to be getting older or weaker. But stars *do* burn out and die after billions of years.

17

On This Page

▶ You might wish to help students understand "life" and "death" as the terms relate to stars. Compare what living things on Earth do (*breathe*, *grow*, *eat*) with what living stars do (*shine*, *burn gases*, *give off light and heat*). Explain that living things on Earth, as well as stars, die when they can no longer carry out essential functions.

▶ Discuss the idea that the words *die* and *live* are opposites. You may also want to point out other opposites, such as *heat/cold* and *light/darkness*.

Cross-Curricular Connections

MATH
Talk about large numbers, such as millions and billions. Write 1,000,000 and 1,000,000,000 on the board, and discuss the idea that one million is one thousand thousands and one billion is one thousand millions. Point out that these numbers are too big for most people to imagine. To help students understand, discuss how many people can be seated in a large place, such as a local stadium, and then figure out how many stadiums would be needed for one million or one billion people.

SCIENCE/MULTICULTURAL
Lead a discussion about the contributions made by various cultures to our understanding of the stars and outer space. Examples include the *gnomons* developed by ancient Chinese astronomers to measure the sun's shadows and the Mayan observatory *el Caracol* at Chichén Itzá in Mexico. Invite students to share their knowledge about how people in their home cultures use the stars for religious, astrological, or timekeeping purposes.

LANGUAGE ARTS
Point out that some words have multiple meanings. Have students consider two definitions of the word *star*: "a celestial body" and "a top performer." Encourage them to discuss other words with multiple meanings, such as *can* ("able to"/"metal container"), *die* ("stop living"/"cube"), *palm* ("inside of hand"/"kind of tree"), and *yard* ("enclosed space"/"thirty-six inches").

MUSIC
Play recordings of songs that feature the moon, sun, stars, or planets. (Examples: "By the Light of the Silvery Moon" or "Here Comes the Sun") Encourage students to make up their own songs, rhymes, or chants about stars. For example, to the tune of "Twinkle, Twinkle, Little Star" they might sing: *Shine and sparkle little star/You look bright from oh so far!/ After many, many years/You'll burn out and disappear. (Repeat the first two lines.)*

Mainstream Connections
Because few students will know as much about black holes as yours will at the end of the theme, you may want individuals to invite mainstream friends to class at that time for an information session designed to shed light on black holes.

On This Page
▶ Flatten a ball of clay to demonstrate the meaning of the verb *squash*.
▶ You may also wish to make the word *layers* memorable by donning an extra shirt, a vest, a jacket, and a coat. Ask students to name the clothes that make up each layer and to count the layers you have put on.

Language Focus
● Adverbs
● Verbs + *-ing* or infinitives
● Types of sentences
▶ Call students' attention to the last sentence on page 18 and have them find the word that ends in *-ly. (tightly)* Point out that adverbs that tell how usually end in *-ly.* Write *-ly* in large letters on a large sheet of paper. Then write each of the following six words on separate sheets of paper: *tight, quick, light, brave, quiet,* and *loud.* Pass the papers to seven volunteers. Ask the student holding the *-ly* paper to pair up beside each of the others in

As a star's gases burn, they give off light and heat. But when the gas runs out, the star stops burning and begins to die.

As the star cools, the outer layers of the star pull in toward the center. The star squashes into a smaller and smaller ball.

If the star was very small, the star ends up as a cold, dark ball called a black dwarf.

If the star was very big, it keeps squashing inward until it's packed together tighter than anything else in the universe!

Imagine if the earth were crushed until it was the size of a tiny marble. That's how tightly this dead star, a black hole, is packed.

18   Mysteries and the Unknown

turn. Ask each pair to hold up their papers. Then invite volunteers to read aloud the adverb formed by each pair.

▶ On the board, write *The star stops burning and begins to die.* Point out that one of two different kinds of verbs can follow another verb: the *-ing* form or the infinitive (*to* followed by the base form of the verb). Ask volunteers to tell which verb is followed by an *-ing* form and which is followed by an infinitive.

▶ Explain that page 19 shows the four kinds of sentences: *statement, question, exclamation,* and *command.* Have volunteers point out the punctuation at the end of a question *What pulls the star in toward its center with such power?* and an exclamation *Just standing up would be hard work!* Have students explain the difference between the statements on the page and the single command or request *Now imagine the force of gravity near a black hole.* Read an example of each type of sentence, and ask students to listen to your tone of voice. Have them practice appropriate intonation as they repeat them.

What pulls the star in towards its center with such power? It's the same force that pulls you down when you jump up—gravity. You've probably seen films of astronauts, and noticed that they bounce as they walk on the moon. The moon's gravity doesn't pull people down as hard as the earth's gravity does.

If the earth were squashed until it was the size of the moon, gravity on Earth would be even stronger than it is now. Just standing up would be hard work! Now imagine the force of gravity near a black hole. A black hole is so tightly packed that its gravity sucks in everything—even light!

19

On This Page

▶ Invite students to demonstrate the meanings of opposites, such as *push* and *pull, center* and *edge, inside* and *outside,* and *up* and *down.*

▶ Have a volunteer use a ball to show the meanings of the words *bounce* and *gravity.* Explain that astronauts walking on the moon seem to bounce because the moon's gravity is weak.

▶ Help students visualize the meaning of the verb phrase *sucks in* by asking them to think about how a vacuum cleaner picks up dust. Ask students to imagine how it would be to have light "sucked in" in this way.

Everyday Talk

● **Expressing probability**

▶ Point out the word *probably* in the second paragraph on page 19. Ask students whether the author can know for sure that all readers have seen films of astronauts. Help them understand that *probably* expresses a likelihood based on facts known at the time.

▶ Help students list things they think are probably true but do not know for sure. Give them language that they can use to express probability. (*I'm pretty sure that . . . /I think that . . . /I'll bet that . . .*) Help them understand the kinds of situations in which these expressions are appropriate.

▶ You may want students to use expressions of probability to speculate about black holes.

Have students write about natural phenomena that interest them. Some students may want to write about phenomena, like thunder and lightning, that they have personally experienced. Others may wish to tell what they would like to know about quasars or radio waves. Less fluent children might make labeled diagrams, and more fluent children might write detailed paragraphs.

HOME–SCHOOL CONNECTION

Invite students to take home *Mysteries and the Unknown* or a theme-related library book. Encourage them to read and discuss the material with a family member.

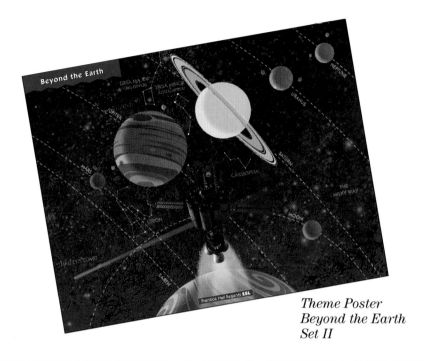

Theme Poster
Beyond the Earth
Set II

On This Page

▶ Invite students to suggest synonyms and antonyms for the word *huge*. (*big, large, enormous, giant, immense/small, tiny, minuscule*)

▶ Have a volunteer reread the first sentence on this page. Help students understand that the word *so* comes between a cause and an effect by asking them to tell which part of the sentence states a cause (*Black holes suck in light*) and which part states an effect (*so we can't see them*).

▶ To help students understand the word *whether*, explain that it signals something and the alternative to that thing.

Black holes suck in light, so we can't see them. Even if you took a huge flashlight and shined it on a black hole, you wouldn't see a thing.

Whenever you see an object, rays of light shine from the object to your eyes. That's true whether you're seeing a wall in a dark room, or the words on this page.

But when rays of light get near a black hole, they don't bounce back. They're sucked into the hole by its powerful gravity. The light from a black hole can never come back to your eyes. Your eyes see nothing but blackness.

20   Mysteries and the Unknown

Language Focus

- **Negative contractions**
- **Homophones**

▶ Explain that a contraction is a word (containing an apostrophe) that is a shortened form of two words. The apostrophe takes the place of letters that were left out when the two words were combined. Tell students that many contractions have been made from negative expressions using the word *not*. Ask them to point out examples on page 20, such as *can't* (*cannot*), *wouldn't* (*would not*), and *don't* (*do not*). You might also point out that not all negative words are contractions.

For instance, on this page both the words *never* and *nothing* are negative.

▶ Explain that homophones are words that sound alike but are spelled differently and have different meanings. Help students find words in the selection that have homophones, such as *to/two/too*, *red/read*, *whole/hole*, *weather/whether*, *know/no*, and *they're/their/there*.

On This Page

▶ To help students comprehend the verb *sway*, have several of them stand in a line and put their hands on the shoulder of their neighbor standing in front of them. Then have the whole group sway slowly back and forth.

▶ Write the word *nothing* on the board. Have students brainstorm creative ways to represent the concept of nothing. Ask them to suggest ways to indicate nothing in a drawing or painting. (*Paint an area black or leave it blank.*)

If black holes are impossible to see, how do we know they're there? Often, we learn about things we *can't* see by the way they affect things we *can* see. We can't see the air, for example. But we can tell it's moving by watching grass sway, or seeing snow swirl around.

Scientists think black holes can move stars, just as the air can move grass.

Stars often swirl around one another. But sometimes scientists see a star that seems to swirl around nothing! When they see a star that seems to swirl around nothing, they think the star might be moving around a black hole!

21

Story Card 2

Language Focus

● **Subject pronouns**

Explain that pronouns are words that take the place of nouns. Point out that we use a pronoun to avoid repeating a name. Have students read the last paragraph on this page and find the subject pronoun that refers to scientists. *(they)*

Everyday Talk

● **Expressing speculation**

▶ Now that students have read a large part of this selection, ask them what they still would like to know about space and stars. Model language to express their speculations. *(I wonder . . . / I'd like to find out . . . /Do you think . . . ?/ Could there be . . . ?)*

▶ Encourage interested students to research answers to the mysteries that they have speculated about. Model language that is commonly used to respond to speculations. *(I'm not sure, but you can probably find a book about that in the library. Maybe this book would help.)*

On This Page

▶ Lead students to understand that we most often use the word *X-ray* to describe a photograph that shows the insides of our bodies. Invite students who have had X-rays taken to describe the experience.

▶ Explain that the word *detect* means "to discover." You might ask them to name a related word that often appears in mystery stories. *(detective)*

BOO!

Scientists also look for black holes by searching for X-rays.

Doctors and dentists pass X-rays through your body to get pictures of your bones and teeth. But X-rays aren't only in doctors' and dentists' offices. Sometimes they're found in space. In particular, scientists believe that when gases get sucked into a black hole, they give off lots of X-rays.

So when scientists see a star swirling around nothing, and detect lots of X-rays, they think that the "nothing" is a mysterious black hole.

22   Mysteries and the Unknown

Theme Project Update

After students finish reading and discussing *The Mystery of Black Holes*, encourage them to think about other ideas for their panel discussion on mysteries. Ideas might include the following:

▶ Create a map or a diagram of the solar system that indicates little known aspects of planets, stars, moons, galaxies, black holes, and white and black dwarfs.

▶ Present illustrations of and brief information about conditions on some of the planets in our solar system and tell what the chances are for life there.

▶ Do research on mysteries, such as UFOs, the statues of Easter Island, or the lost continent of Atlantis.

On This Page

You may wish to give students the following additional facts about black holes: To become a black hole, a star with the diameter of the sun (865,000 miles or 1,392,000 kilometers) would be compressed to a diameter of less than 4 miles (6 kilometers.) Scientists believe that black holes make up as much as a third of the material in the Milky Way (the Earth's galaxy). Huge black holes have been discovered in the center of the Milky Way.

What Did Students Learn?

Encourage students to look at the question tree they began to develop before they read *The Mystery of Black Holes.* Invite volunteers to read aloud any entries they have circled and those they added as they learned more about black holes. Then ask volunteers to answer the questions. Some students may enjoy writing the answers on "twigs" that they add to the tree. Others may want to do further research to find information that will answer unresolved questions.

WRITER'S JOURNAL

Have students think about how it would feel to be in a place where they could see nothing but blackness. Then encourage them to write about those feelings. Help children who wish to dictate their feelings or pair them with a more proficient writer who can record their journal entry.

Scientists can tell where black holes are. The real mystery is what it's like inside a black hole.

But getting into a black hole wouldn't be easy! First you'd have to travel billions of miles through space to reach one. As you got near the black hole, its gravity would stretch you way, way out.

If you could stand the stretching and enter the black hole, no one knows what it would be like inside. Time might stand still. Or time might go backward. You might even find yourself in a tunnel to another universe!

But whatever you found out, you wouldn't be able to tell your friends; nothing that enters a black hole can ever leave—including you!

23

After You Read

Post-Reading Activities

OBJECTIVES

● LISTENING/SPEAKING To give a synopsis
● WRITING To write a summary

Vocabulary Check

Have small groups of students use the illustrations in the reading selection to give synopses of what they learned about black holes. Have each group choose a page and then use the art on the page to tell what explanation of black holes they derived from reading the selection. You may want to help volunteers in each group list the key vocabulary words on the board before the groups start their synopses in order to encourage them to use the new vocabulary.

Practice

Use Story Card 2 to help students practice using vocabulary relating to stars, space, and black holes. Invite individual students to imagine that each one is the person in the picture. What would each student write in a notebook? Have pairs of students work together to fill out a sheet of notebook paper labeled "Stars That I've Seen." You may want to pair less fluent with more fluent students. Encourage them to use illustrations and to name stars in their first languages if they don't know the English names.

Comprehension Check

▶ Urge students to talk about the picture on page 25. Then have them work in pairs to complete the activity. As they work, students may find it helpful to discuss other facts and concepts they learned from reading the story.

▶ To reinforce vocabulary and concepts taught in this theme, have students look at Transparency 4. You may want to ask a volunteer to point to the black hole. Then ask questions relating to black holes, such as: *How can you tell there is a black hole there? Can you see it? What is a black hole?* Have students identify and discuss other parts of the illustration, including astronauts, Earth, the moon, the sun, and the stars.

Looking Back at the Story

To help summarize information about the challenging subject of black holes, have students dictate to you what they consider to be the most important facts they learned. Record those facts on chart paper.

Everyday Talk

● **Making guesses**

▶ Have students look at the cartoon at the bottom of page 25 while two volunteers read the text. Model Scooter's answer and then have students repeat the expressions in the box.

▶ Ask students to discuss in pairs the question *What do you think Daisy and Scooter see?* Encourage them to use the expressions in the box. After a few minutes, have the class come together to make a list of their guesses. Their guesses may include additional "mystery" vocabulary, such as *flying saucer* and *UFO*.

▶ Use classroom objects that students may be familiar with to play a guessing game. Fill the bag with as many items as there are students in the class. Then blindfold a volunteer. Have that student choose an item from the bag and then identify it by feeling its size and shape. Encourage the student to describe the object as he or she handles it. (*It's long and thin. It has a point at one end. The other end is soft. Maybe it's a pencil.*) Encourage students who might not know the name of an object to describe its use or pantomime using it. (*It's what you use to make the writing on paper go away.*)

So next time you stare up at the night sky, remember: there's more in the sky than meets the eye! Scattered in the silent darkness are black holes—the great mystery of space.

24 Mysteries and the Unknown

Evaluate

On the board, write a concept web featuring a black hole in the center. On lines emanating from the center, write questions that will help you analyze students' comprehension of the reading. Have students read the questions aloud and answer them.

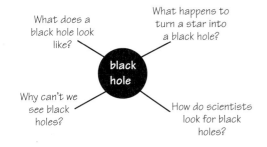

Beginning

● To label a mural

PRE-WRITE: Have students talk about the things that a space traveler might see in outer space. *(planets, stars, the moon, astronauts, spaceships, the sun, swirling stars)* Then have them work together to paint a mural that shows all the things they mentioned. WRITE: Give students stick-on labels or note cards, and ask them to write a label for each thing in the mural. REVISE, EDIT: Have students check one another's work and revise as necessary. PUBLISH: Hang the mural and have students attach their labels near the corresponding pictures.

Intermediate

● To write a description

PRE-WRITE: As the beginning group of students creates its mural, ask the intermediate group to talk with them about what they are showing. WRITE: Ask each student to choose a different object that is taking shape in the mural and to write a brief description of it. REVISE, EDIT: Have students share first drafts with one another and revise as they wish. Then ask them to write final drafts on a computer. PUBLISH: Exhibit the descriptions by hanging them around the mural and taping brightly colored yarn from the descriptions to the objects they describe.

Advanced

● To write a proposal

PRE-WRITE: Have students imagine that they are going to enter a Young Astronomers contest. Encourage them to think about a mystery of space that they would like to explore. Then ask them to make lists of scientific investigations that they could do to solve their mysteries. WRITE: Ask students to write a proposal that tells what they want to research and investigate, why their research project is important, and how they intend to carry it out. REVISE, EDIT: Have each student read his or her proposal to one or more classmates to see whether the ideas are clear and convincing. After making changes recommended by the audience, the student should exchange papers with another student to read and correct grammar and spelling errors, if any, and to revise as necessary. PUBLISH: Have students collect their essays in a folder for the classroom resource center.

For coordinating activities, see the CD-ROM disk that corresponds with this theme.

Real-Life Reading

Mysteries of the World

READING STRATEGIES
CRITICAL THINKING SKILLS

- Recalling information
- Drawing conclusions
- Making judgments about the credibility of sources

OBJECTIVES

- **READING** To activate background knowledge/To predict content using illustrations and headlines
- **LISTENING/SPEAKING** To tell about one's own experiences/To participate in a panel discussion/To solve a riddle
- **WRITING** To write a news headline/To complete a newspaper article/To write a group mystery story
- **CULTURAL** To share mysteries from one's home culture
- **STUDY SKILLS** To research information

KEY VOCABULARY

triangle, sphinx, pyramid, riddle, cave, wheel, secrets, unidentified flying object (UFO), crop, field, design, solve, bent, destroyed, ancient, amateur, surprised, strange, normally, reportedly

Mysterious Places

Pre-Reading Have students scan page 26 and tell where each pictured place is located. Ask what all the places have in common. *(Each place is mysterious in some way.)* Be sure that students understand that this page of the magazine feature shows places that really exist.

▶ You may wish to use questions such as the following to help students familiarize themselves with the vocabulary represented in the pictures:

Point to a pyramid. **(PREPODUCTION)** *Which shape is shown on the map, a triangle or a circle?* **(EARLY PRODUCTION)** *What does the head of the statue look like? What does its body look like?* **(SPEECH EMERGENCE)** *Which place would you like to visit? Why?* **(NEARLY-FLUENT)**

Reading Ask volunteers to read the descriptions of the three pictures of mysterious places. Encourage students to guess the meanings of unfamiliar words from contextual and visual clues.

▶ Point out the word *mysterious* and ask students what noun this adjective comes from. Discuss what makes each place seem mysterious.

▶ Ask students why they think the Great Sphinx was built near the pyramids at Giza. Then tell them that people believe it guarded the pyramids, which were the tombs of the pharaohs.

▶ Have students read the riddle of the ancient Greek sphinx in the caption and discuss possible answers. Point out that they will solve the riddle at the end of the theme.

▶ Next, point out the description of the Bighorn Medicine Wheel. Ask students what scientists think the wheel was used for. Invite students to think of other possible uses. Ask them to tell what clues the picture gives.

Post-Reading Invite students to choose which of the three pictured places they would prefer to visit. Divide the class into three groups based on their selections. Have each group discuss why they would like to visit their chosen location. Working together, each group should come up with a list of reasons to present to the class. After all three groups have presented their reasons, ask the class if the reasons made anyone want to change his or her choice.

▶ Ask students to work in small groups to create a description of a mysterious place in their home country or in their community. Post the description in class. You may wish to encourage a class discussion comparing and contrasting these places.

- Have pairs of students work together on Activity Page 4. Guide more fluent students to help less fluent ones.
- Use Story Card 3 to present and discuss one more mystery of the world: the statues of Easter Island. Have students compare and contrast this mystery with those shown on page 26.

In the News

Pre-Reading Find out what students know about UFOs. Discuss the issue of eyewitness accounts versus scientific evidence. Ask: *Which article is more likely to be true?*

- If possible, bring in sample newspaper headlines, preferably dealing with mysterious phenomena, like aliens from space. (Tabloid newspapers are a good source.) Invite students to tell about any similar headlines they have seen in their home languages or in English. Point out that headlines are designed to attract a reader's attention and to give an idea of what the article is about. Add that tabloid headlines are meant to excite people and are not necessarily true.

Reading Before students read the articles on page 27, have them read the headlines and look at the photos to predict what the articles are about. Then encourage the class to offer possible explanations for the events. Ask: *Do you think these articles refer to real events? What part(s) of each story may be fact? How can we explain things that are not factual?*

- Have students identify and read silently the ad on page 27. Discuss why someone might want to research UFOs. *(to find out whether there are UFOs or where and when they are most likely to be reported)*

Post-Reading Have students tell how they would complete the two newspaper articles on page 27. Less fluent students can act out or describe orally how the stories might continue. More fluent students can write out the rest of the articles and read them aloud to the class.

- Invite students to write their own newspaper headline about a mysterious event they have heard about or imagined. Encourage them to make their headlines short, to the point, and attention-getting.

IN THE NEWS

Sixth-Grader Spots UFO

Middletown—USA A 12-year-old amateur astronomer reported spotting an unidentified flying object through her telescope last night. Emily Rodriguez, who is in the sixth grade at John Dewey Middle School, saw a large glowing object moving slowly through the sky at around 9:15 p.m.

Police say they received a number of calls from curious residents between 9:10 and 9:20 p.m. Most callers described an unusually large, reddish-orange light in the sky.

"I was very surprised," said the young astronomer. "I was looking for Saturn."

Classified

Have you seen a UFO?

Participants needed for scientific research project on UFOs. You will be paid.

Call 555-2792

Serious replies only, please.

Scientists Can't Explain Crop Circles

FRANKLIN—Local farmers have been finding huge circles and other designs that reportedly have appeared overnight in their fields. In most cases, crops have been bent—but not destroyed—to form the designs. Some of the designs cover an area as large as three football fields.

"It's definitely not the sort of thing you see every day out here," says Roy Perry. His hayfield looks as if someone had mowed an enormous circle through it, yet the alfalfa itself has not been cut or damaged in any way. In fact, Perry's crop continues to grow normally. "What's weird is that there aren't any tire tracks or anything, and it would have taken a pretty big machine to do this job," he adds.

27

Story Card 3

Everyday Talk

- Expressing disbelief
- Expressing surprise

▶ Read the cartoon strip on page 28 with appropriate intonation. Encourage students to tell what is happening in each frame. Then ask three volunteers to reread the conversation.

▶ Have other volunteers read aloud the expressions in the box. Encourage students to use dramatic intonation, facial expression, and other gestures.

▶ Have pairs role-play conversations in which people show disbelief or surprise.

Extension Activities

▶ More fluent students may enjoy extending the conversation among the three characters in the cartoon strip.

▶ Have students research surprising events. Provide sources like *Ripley's Believe It or Not* and *The Guinness Book of World Records*. Ask each student to report one interesting surprise to the class. After all the reports have been given, have the class vote on the most surprising event and the most mysterious event.

Story Card 4

Here and There

Mysterious Pyramids

▶ Have students look at the illustrations on page 29 and ask a volunteer to read the captions. If students have visited any pyramids, ask them to share their memories of the experience. Students may also have historical information to share about pyramids.

▶ Next, have students read the paragraphs. Encourage them to answer the questions using details they see in the pictures as well as what they already know about pyramids and different cultures.

▶ Tell students that pyramids were built by ancient civilizations in Mexico, Central America, Iraq, and Egypt. The pyramids served as temples and tombs for kings, queens, and other important people. In some cultures, the pyramids were meant to protect the dead in the life after death.

Egyptian Pyramids The most famous pyramids in Egypt are near the city of Giza, west of the Nile River. This group of pyramids is one of the Seven Wonders of the Ancient World, seven sights that ancient travelers thought were especially important to see. The pyramid of Khufu, or the Great Pyramid, was built for King Khufu of Egypt (or Cheops, as the ancient Greeks called him). It is the tallest pyramid ever built. More than two million blocks of stone, each one weighing more than $2\frac{1}{2}$ tons, were used to build it. It originally stood 756 feet high.

Mexican Pyramid The pyramid at Chichén Itzá stands in the central Yucatán peninsula in Mexico. It is part of a large complex of buildings constructed by the Maya and other ancient peoples. A temple to the gods, the pyramid is embellished with very detailed carvings of Quetzalcoatl and other mythical figures. (For the legend of Quetzalcoatl, the plumed serpent, see *Marvelous Myths* in this series.)

Extension Activity

Students may enjoy making three-dimensional models of pyramids. Make a large pattern like the example below. Students can trace this pattern onto heavy paper or posterboard. Then they can cut out the pattern, fold along the edges, and tape or glue the tabs indicated by the dotted lines.

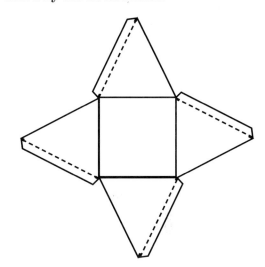

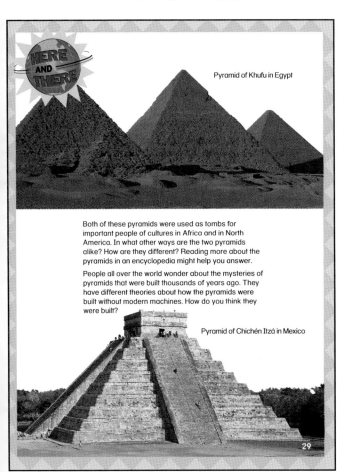

Pyramid of Khufu in Egypt

Both of these pyramids were used as tombs for important people of cultures in Africa and in North America. In what other ways are the two pyramids alike? How are they different? Reading more about the pyramids in an encyclopedia might help you answer.

People all over the world wonder about the mysteries of pyramids that were built thousands of years ago. They have different theories about how the pyramids were built without modern machines. How do you think they were built?

Pyramid of Chichén Itzá in Mexico

Theme Project

▦ Have students read page 30 and encourage them to talk about the questions. Then have the panel discussion groups use the page to evaluate their own work.

▸ After doing the evaluation on page 30, groups may want to revise or add to their panel discussions before they hold them in class. Allow groups extra time to do this.

▸ When groups are ready to hold their panel discussions, arrange to have a volunteer record them on video or audio tape. Encourage the audience to ask each panel questions about their presentation.

Extension Activities

▦ Have students create a *Big Book of Mystery* for younger children. Inspire the class to think up a simple plot: a place, an event, and two or three characters. Remind students that the story must have a clear beginning, middle, and end and should not be too scary for its young audience.

Encourage students to make a first draft by writing sentences and/or drawing pictures on $8\frac{1}{2}$-by-11-inch paper. Have them work together to revise the story. Then have them copy the final draft onto much larger paper for the big book. Each page should have an illustration and one or

two sentences written in large print. When all the pages are finished, bind them together to make the big book. If possible, arrange to read it to a kindergarten or first-grade class.

▸ After students have seen or heard recordings of their panel discussions and have done the self-assessment activities on page 31 of the Teacher's Edition, they may feel confident enough to hold their discussions in a mainstream class.

What You Might See

See Theme Project Update, page 23.

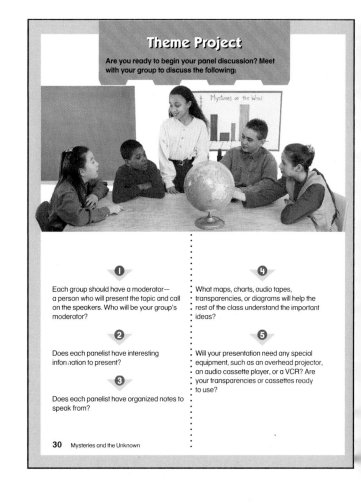

Theme Project

Are you ready to begin your panel discussion? Meet with your group to discuss the following:

❶ Each group should have a moderator— a person who will present the topic and call on the speakers. Who will be your group's moderator?

❷ Does each panelist have interesting information to present?

❸ Does each panelist have organized notes to speak from?

❹ What maps, charts, audio tapes, transparencies, or diagrams will help the rest of the class understand the important ideas?

❺ Will your presentation need any special equipment, such as an overhead projector, an audio cassette player, or a VCR? Are your transparencies or cassettes ready to use?

30 Mysteries and the Unknown

Theme Wrap-Up

Theme Puzzle

▶ Have students work individually or in pairs to complete the sentences.

▶ Help the class unscramble the answer to the riddle. Lead a discussion of why it is a good answer. Be sure to explain that human beings crawl when they are babies, walk on two legs when they grow up, and may use a cane to help them walk when they get older.

Oral Review

To give students added practice with theme vocabulary, use Story Card 4 and the theme poster. You may also wish to revisit the transparencies and/or the cards from Parts 1 and 2.

Self-Assessment

▶ Play the video or the audio tape recording of students' panel discussions. Invite students to evaluate their own performances and those of other groups by asking themselves questions such as the following:

How did I help my group this time?
How could I help my group work better next time?
What could the other groups learn from my group about working together?
What could my group learn from the other groups about working together?

Shy or less fluent students might benefit from a private discussion with you rather than speaking in front of classmates. Suggest that students write down their answers and refer to them the next time they do a group presentation or activity.

▶ Write some of the theme's key concepts on the board, and ask students to think about what they learned from their work on *Mysteries and the Unknown*. Give each student a copy of a chart with the follow-ing headings: *What I Learned, What Was Interesting, What Was Fun, What I Did Best*, and *What I Need to Do Better*. Suggest that students try articulating their thoughts to a partner before writing them in the chart. (You may wish to pair up speakers who have the same home language—one who is more fluent in English and one who is less fluent.) When the charts are completed, encourage volunteers to discuss their responses with the whole class. You may wish to generate and post a class chart based on the discussion.

> **What I Learned**
> A detective solves mysteries.
> There are black holes in space.
>
> **What Was Interesting**
> I liked reading about the pyramids.
> I wonder how people built them.
>
> **What Was Fun**
> Reading the newspaper article about the UFO was fun.
>
> **What I Did Best**
> I solved the theme puzzle!
>
> **What I Need to Do Better**
> To be a better panelist, I need to speak louder.

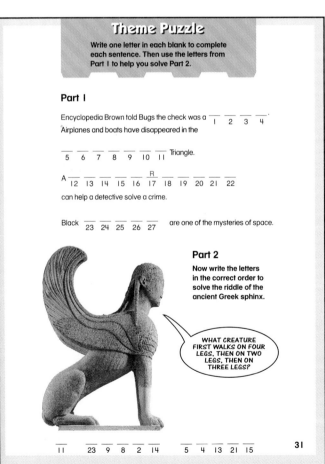

Theme Puzzle

Write one letter in each blank to complete each sentence. Then use the letters from Part I to help you solve Part 2.

Part I

Encyclopedia Brown told Bugs the check was a — — — — .
1 2 3 4

Airplanes and boats have disappeared in the

— — — — — — — Triangle.
5 6 7 8 9 10 11

A — — — R — — — — — —
12 13 14 15 16 17 18 19 20 21 22
can help a detective solve a crime.

Black — — — — — are one of the mysteries of space.
23 24 25 26 27

Part 2

Now write the letters in the correct order to solve the riddle of the ancient Greek sphinx.

> WHAT CREATURE FIRST WALKS ON FOUR LEGS, THEN ON TWO LEGS, THEN ON THREE LEGS?

— — — — — — — — — — — —
11 23 9 8 2 14   5 4 13 21 15

31

Theme Bibliography

▶ Adler, David A. *Cam Jansen and the Mystery of the Stolen Corn Popper.* Viking Kestrel, 1986. This title is one in an easy-reading series about a fifth-grade girl detective who uses her photographic memory to catch a thief in a department store.

▶ Asimov, Isaac. *Quasars, Pulsars, and Black Holes.* Isaac Asimov's Library of the Universe. Gareth Stevens, 1988. Written for young readers by a well-known scientist, this book discusses facts and theories about these three outer space phenomena.

▶ Branley, Franklyn M. *Journey into a Black Hole.* Let's-Read-and-Find-Out Science Book. Thomas Y. Crowell, 1986. The reader is taken on an exciting imaginary journey through a black hole.

▶ Cushman, Doug. *Aunt Eater's Mystery Vacation.* An I Can Read Book (for beginning readers). HarperCollins, 1992. In this amusing story, an anteater solves mysteries during her vacation at Hotel Bathwater.

▶ Hess, Debra. *Escape from Earth.* The Spy from Outer Space Series. Hyperion Paperbacks for Children, 1994. In this story, which combines mystery and science fiction, Cassie and her friend, Zeke, a boy from outer space, try to find the meaning of a mysterious message that has been left on Zeke's spaceship.

▶ Keyishian, Amy and Elizabeth. *Digging for Clues.* Ghostwriter Series. A Children's Television Workshop Book. Bantam Books, 1994. Two girls want to discover what's buried beneath Fort Greene. Something buried there is so valuable that a new supermarket can't be built on the site.

▶ Stine, R. L. *Let's Get Invisible!* Goosebumps Series. Scholastic, 1993. In the attic, a boy finds a magic mirror that can make him invisible. Then he finds that he's losing control of his magic power. R. L. Stine is the author of more than two dozen best-selling mysteries for young people.

See also the Professional Bibliography in the Teacher's Companion.

PRENTICE HALL REGENTS
A VIACOM COMPANY

© 1996 by Prentice Hall Regents
Prentice Hall Inc.
A Viacom Company
Upper Saddle River, NJ 07458

Prentice Hall Regents
Publisher: Marilyn Lindgren
Development Editors: Carol Callahan, Fredrik Liljeblad, Kathleen Ossip
Assistant Editor: Susan Frankle
Director of Production: Aliza Greenblatt
Manufacturing Buyer: Dave Dickey
Production Coordinator: Ken Liao
Marketing Manager: Richard Seltzer

Editorial, Design, Production and Packaging
McClanahan & Company, Inc.
Project Director: Susan Cornell Poskanzer
Creative Director: Lisa Olsson
Design Director: Toby Carson
Director of Production: Karen Pekarne

TEACHER'S EDITION
Illustration: Tim Haggerty, cover; Dartmouth Publishing p1
Photography: Ken Karp Photography p21, p30

STORY CARDS
Illustration: Barbara Gray SC1; Joe Boddy SC2; Donald Mulligan SC3; Stephanie K. Birdsong SC4

THEME POSTER
Illustration: Joe Van Der Bos

Reduced Student Book art is credited in Student Book.

All rights reserved. No part of this book may be reproduced, in any form or by any means, without permission in writing from the publisher.

Printed in the United States of America

10 9 8 7 6 5 4 3

ISBN 0-13-367236-0

Prentice-Hall International (UK) Limited, London
Prentice-Hall of Australia Pty. Limited, Sydney
Prentice-Hall Canada Inc., Toronto
Prentice-Hall Hispanoamericana, S.A., Mexico
Prentice-Hall of India Private Limited, New Delhi
Prentice-Hall of Japan, Inc., Tokyo
Simon & Schuster Asia Pte. Ltd., Singapore
Editora Prentice-Hall do Brasil, Ltda., Rio de Janeiro